EVERYBODY FEELS FEAR!

BY ASHWIN CHACKO

EVERYBODY FEELS FEAR!

written and illustrated by
ASHWIN CHACKO

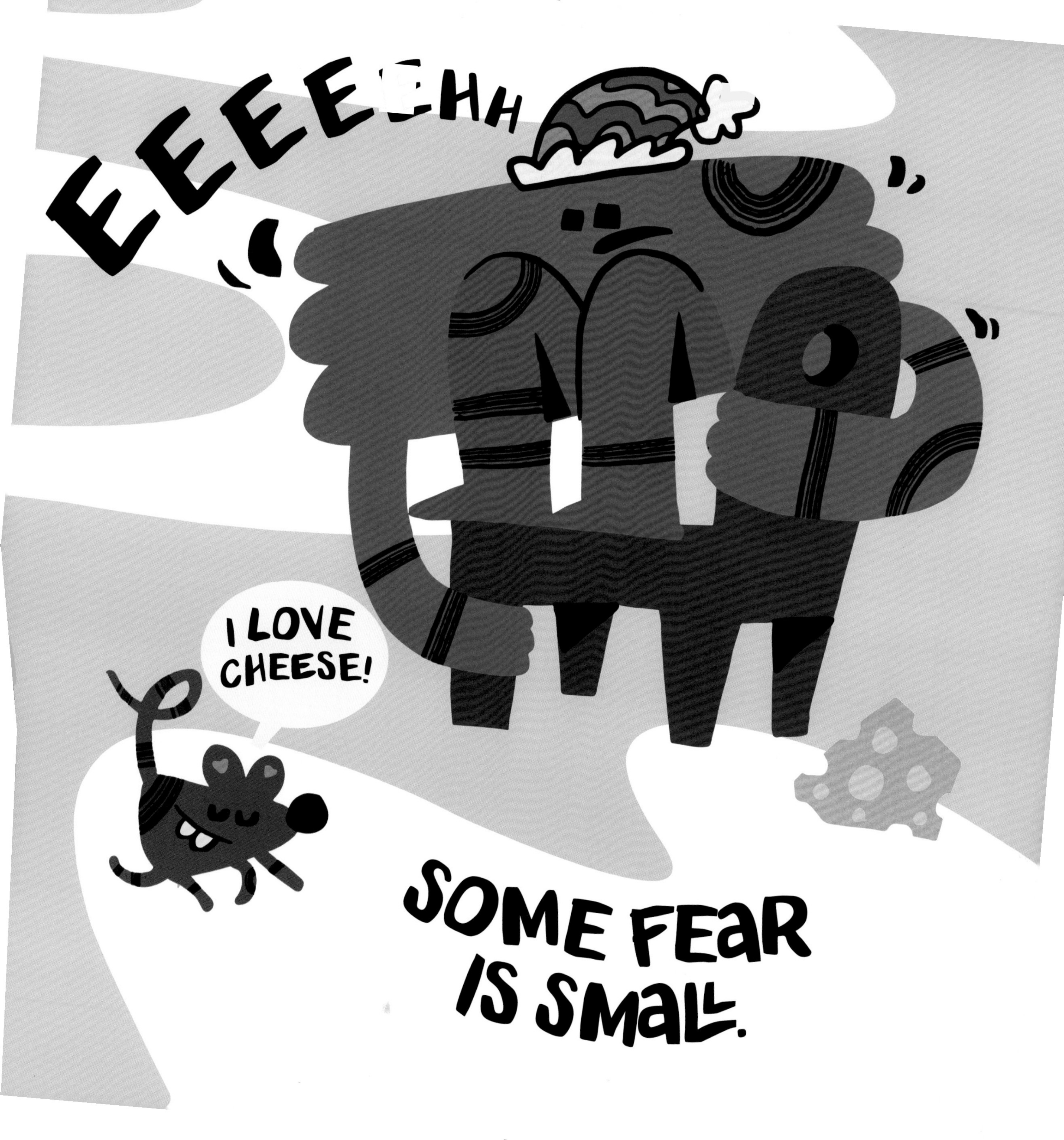

SOME FEAR IS SMALL.

SOME FEAR CAN EVEN INVOLVE HONEY.

WE ALL FEEL **FEAR**, NO MATTER HOW YOUNG OR OLD.

SOME FEAR
IS SCARY.

SOME FEAR
IS IN THE
DARK.

WE ALL FEEL **FEAR,** NO MATTER IF YOU ARE NERDY OR COOL.

FEAR CAN OVERWHELM US.
EVERYONE FEELS IT.
NO ONE ESCAPES.

Fear might seem like it covers the whole world.

TO BE BRAVE IS
NOT TO BE UNAFRAID,
BUT TO MOVE FORWARD
EVEN WHEN IT SEEMS
SCARY.

WE ARE BUILT
TO BE STRONG,
BRILLIANTLY
CREATED TO
STAND UP TO
FEAR
AND SAY
NO.

FEAR DOES NOT DEFINE YOU—

EVEN IN THE HARDEST MOMENTS, ON THE HARDEST DAYS.

DIG DEEP AND SEE WHO YOU ARE MADE TO BE—

Brave FEaRLESS

PERFECTLY LOVED, WITH A RIGHT TO PEACE.

LOVE IS THE FUEL OF COURAGE, FOR IT COMPELS US INTO ACTION.

AND WHERE LOVE LIVES, FEAR CANNOT BE—FOR LOVE REJECTS ALL FEAR.

ASHWIN CHACKO IS AN INDIAN AUTHOR, ILLUSTRATOR, AND MOTIVATIONAL SPEAKER BASED IN DUBLIN. HE SPECIALIZES IN POSITIVELY PLAYFUL, VISUAL STORYTELLING TO BRING JOY AND ENCOURAGEMENT.

HIS MISSION IS TO CHAMPION CREATIVITY AND EMPOWER PEOPLE TO FIND THEIR INNER SPARK THROUGH HIS ART, BOOKS, TALKS, & WORKSHOPS.

Penguin
Random
House

First American Edition, 2022
Published in the United States by DK Publishing
1745 Broadway, 20th Floor, New York, NY 10019

Text and illustrations copyright © Ashwin Chacko, 2022
Layouts and design copyright © Dorling Kindersley Limited, 2022
DK, a Division of Penguin Random House LLC
19 20 21 22 23 10 9 8 7 6 5 4 3 2 1
001–331772–Nov/2022

A catalog record for this book
is available from the Library of Congress.
ISBN: 978-0-7440-6262-5

DK books are available at special discounts when purchased in bulk for sales promotions, premiums, fund-raising, or educational use.
For details, contact: DK Publishing Special Markets,
1745 Broadway, 20th Floor, New York, NY 10019
SpecialSales@dk.com

Printed and bound in China

For the curious
www.dk.com

MIX
Paper from
responsible sources
FSC™ C018179